Robert Schumann

Great Works for Piano and Orchestra in Full Score

Concerto in A Minor, Op. 54

Concertstück (Introduction and Allegro appassionato), Op. 92

Introduction and Allegro, Op. 134

FROM THE COMPLETE WORKS EDITION
EDITED BY
Clara Schumann

DOVER PUBLICATIONS, INC.
New York

Published in Canada by General Publishing Company, Ltd., 30 Lesmill Road, Don Mills, Toronto, Ontario.
Published in the United Kingdom by Constable and Company, Ltd., 10 Orange Street, London WC2H 7EG.

This Dover edition, first published in 1982, contains three works from *Serie III. Concerte and Concertstücke für Orchester* of the complete works edition *Robert Schumann's Werke. Herausgegeben von Clara Schumann* (original publication years: *Piano Concerto,* 1883; *Concertstück,* 1884; *Introduction and Allegro,* 1887). The Contents and the Glossary of German Terms are new elements specially prepared for the present edition.

International Standard Book Number: 0-486-24340-0

Manufactured in the United States of America
Dover Publications, Inc.
180 Varick Street
New York, N.Y. 10014

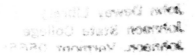

CONTENTS

GLOSSARY
of German Terms Occurring on the Music Pages

bewegter: more agitatedly; "più agitato"

Bratsche: viola

Cadenz: cadenza

Clarinetten in B: B-flat clarinets

Contrabass: double bass, string bass

das Tempo nach und nach beschleunigen bis . . . : gradually accelerate the tempo up to . . .

die ♩ wie vorher die ♩ : ♩ = the previous ♩

ein Cello allein: solo cello

etwas zurückhaltend: holding back somewhat

Fagotte: bassoons

Flöten: flutes

gehalten zu spielen: to be played "sostenuto"

getheilt: "divisi"

Hoboen: oboes

im Tempo: in tempo; "a tempo"

langsam: slowly

lebhaft: vivaciously; "vivace"

markirt: "marcato"

mit: with

mit (aller) Kraft: with (full) force

mit freiem Vortrag: freely

nach und nach: gradually

ohne: without

Pauken in E.H.: kettledrums tuned in E and B

schneller: faster

sehr: very

Tenor-Posaune: tenor trombone

und: and

(Ventil)hörner: (valve) horns

(Ventil)trompeten: (valve) trumpets

Verschiebung: soft pedal

Violine: violin

Violoncell: cello

ziemlich: rather, fairly

Piano Concerto in A Minor, Op. 54

Piano Concerto in A Minor,
Op. 54

SOLO.

INTERMEZZO.

Allegro vivace.

Allegro vivace.

Allegro vivace.

60 Piano Concerto in A Minor

72   Piano Concerto in A Minor

94 Piano Concerto in A Minor

Concertstück
(Introduction and Allegro appassionato), Op. 92

Concertstück (Introduction and Allegro appassionato), Op. 92

128 Concertstück

muta in D.

Introduction and Allegro,
Op. 134

Introduction and Allegro, Op. 134

Solo

Solo